Holidays & Festivals

JEWISH FESTIVALS

Reuben Turner

Rourke Enterprises, Inc.
Vero Beach, FL 32964

Holidays and Festivals

Christmas
Thanksgiving and Harvest
New Year
Jewish Festivals
Muslim Festivals
Buddhist Festivals

Library of Congress Cataloging-in-Publication Data

Turner, Reuben.
Jewish festivals.

(Holidays and festivals)
Bibliography: p.
Includes index.
Summary: Explains the origins of major Jewish festivals and how they are celebrated.
1. Fasts and feasts — Judaism — Juvenile literature.
[1. Fasts and feasts — Judaism. 2. Judaism — Customs and practices] I. Title. II. Series.
BM690.T87 1987 296.4'3 87-4325
ISBN 0-86592-977-7

First published in the United States in 1987 by Rourke Enterprises, Inc.
Vero Beach, FL 32964

Photoset by Direct Image Photosetting
Printed in Italy by G. Canale & C.S.p.A., Turin

Contents

Passover

The Freedom Festival

For hundreds of years, Jewish boys and girls have asked the same question at the ceremony that marks the beginning of the Passover festival: "Why is this night different from all other nights?" This special night in the Jewish calendar, probably the most popular event in the year for Jewish children all over the world, is known as Seder night. The word Seder means "order" or "arrangement," and the whole ceremony is arranged in a special order of events.

Passover is a festival that celebrates many things. First and foremost, it celebrates the time when the Jewish people were released from their many years of slavery in Egypt and became a free nation. It is also an agricultural festival, marking the beginning of the grain harvest during the time the Jews lived in the Holy Land. Passover is also a pilgrim festival, as it is one of the three occasions when, according to the commandments of the *Torah* (see page 16), the Israelites went in joyous procession to Jerusalem. The other two occasions were on the main festivals of *Shavuot* and *Tabernacles.*

The name "Passover" is derived from the Hebrew word *pesach,* which means to "pass over,"

A fifteenth-century painting of Jews celebrating the Passover.

referring to the night when the Almighty passed over the houses of the Jews on his way to slay the first-born males of the Egyptians.

We have to turn the clock back many hundreds of years to learn briefly of the story of Passover. At one time, the Jewish people – who became known as the Israelites – were living in Egypt. After a number of years, a new Pharaoh came to power and made the Israelites his slaves.

The most important ceremony at Passover is the Seder. Seder night marks the beginning of the Passover festival.

After the tenth plague, the Pharaoh begged Moses to take the Israelites out of Egypt.

After many years of slavery, God appeared to an Israelite called Moses and told him to go to the Pharaoh, together with his brother Aaron, and ask him to free the Israelites from slavery. Moses and Aaron pleaded with the Pharaoh, but to no avail. God then struck the Egyptians with a series of plagues. After the tenth plague, the killing of the Egyptian children by the Almighty, Pharaoh called Moses and begged him to take the Israelites out of Egypt.

Immediately, Moses gathered the Jews together and told them to prepare for their departure from Egypt into the Wilderness to become a free

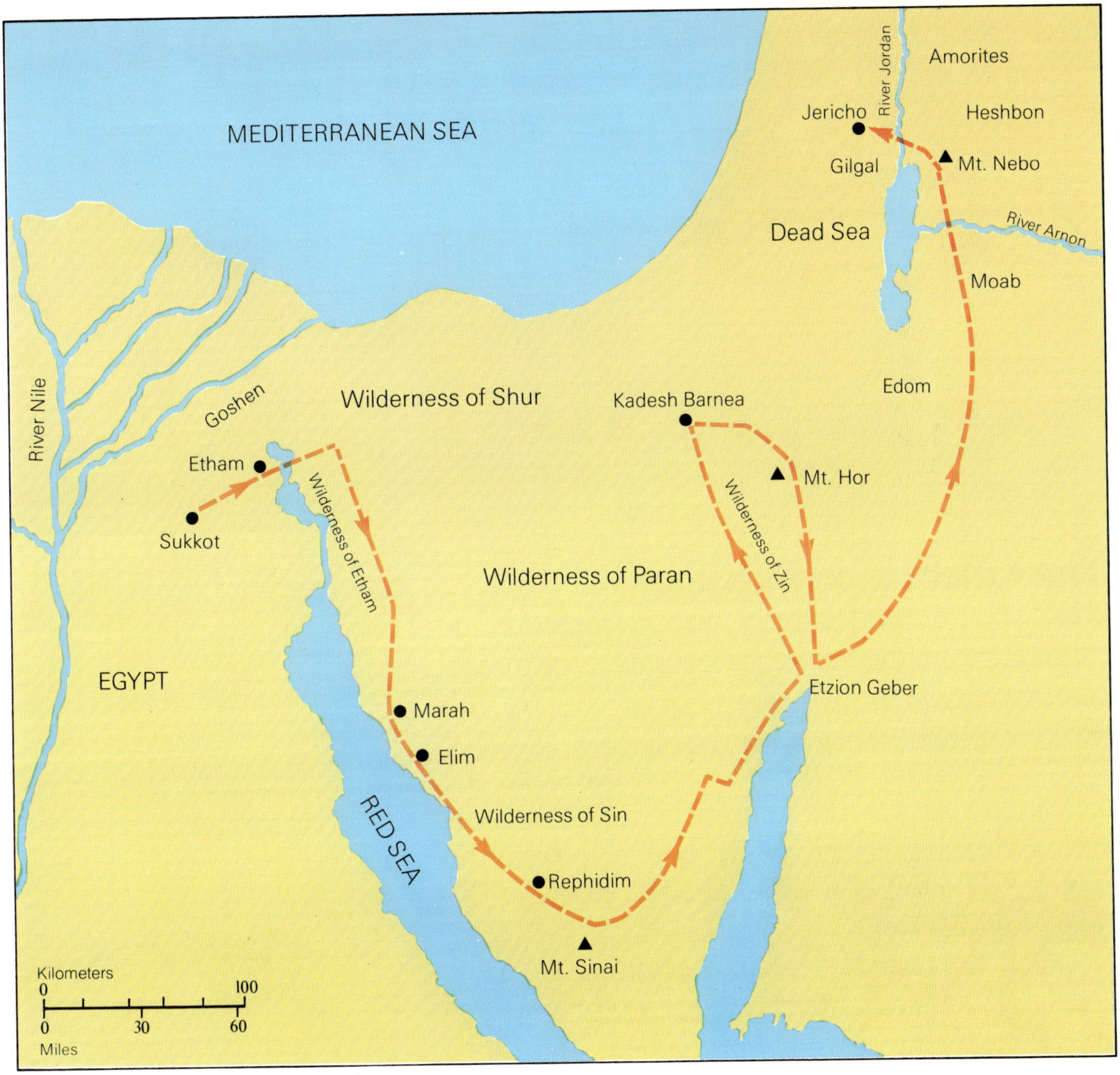

people. Everything was done with speed and abruptness. They made offerings of lamb to God and baked *Matzah*, unleavened bread, as there was no time to let the dough rise. This was the beginning of the Exodus – the escape from slavery – and the beginning of the Jewish nation, although they were not yet in their own land.

A map of the Exodus – the route Moses and the Israelites took through the Wilderness after leaving Egypt.

The search for leaven has always preceded the Passover festival.

The Celebration Service

Weeks before the Passover festival, preparations commence in the home by cleaning the house from top to bottom in order to make sure that no leaven – food that contains yeast, such as bread – will be found in the house by the time the festival arrives. So the housewife does a kind of spring-cleaning, usually with some help from the rest of the family, in order for the house to be ready for Passover.

When the festival begins, everything is clean; special dishes and cutlery used only for Passover are on the Seder table, and everyone is dressed in their best clothes. In a happy and excited mood the father, mother and family take their places around the table, the father seated at the head. Everyone has a copy of a special book, called the *Haggadah*, which recalls the Exodus and gives the text for the order of this celebration service.

In front of the father are the items to be eaten during the service – foods that will remind those present of the events that took place all those years ago:

- The thin, wafer-like *Matzah,* which is known as "the bread of slavery and affliction."
- The bitter herbs (usually horseradish) eaten as a reminder of the bitter times experienced by the Israelites in Egypt.
- Fresh green lettuce as a sign of spring.
- Cups of wine as a symbol of liberty and joy.
- The mixture of apples, nuts, cinnamon and wine called *Charoset,* which looks like cement and represents the bricks and mortar used by the Israelites to build the palaces and cities in Egypt.

The cushions on the chairs are a symbol of freedom and relaxation in contrast to slavery and oppression.

All the food and drink you can see on the Seder table has a special meaning.

The Passover Message

Passover is not just a reminder of past Jewish history. It is also about the present and the future of the Jewish people. It serves as a constant reminder of the importance of freedom to each individual. In fact, the first of the Ten Commandments opens with a reference to it: "I am the Lord your God who brought you out of the Land of

This beautiful stained-glass window showing the Seder table can be seen in the Central Synagogue, London.

Everyone at the Seder table has a copy of the Haggadah, *the book that tells the story of the Exodus and God's delivery of the Israelites from slavery to freedom.*

Egypt, out of the house of bondage.'' Thus, for Jews, freedom is declared by God to be man's birthright.

This festival, known also as the Festival of Spring, occurs around the months of March and April, and indicates hope for a world of peace and plenty for all mankind. In the spring we see vegetation come to life again and the start of a new cycle of agricultural activity after the winter. Similarly, this spring festival conveys to the Jews the everlasting message of the importance of starting life afresh, as well as of being free.

Recipes

Why not try to make *Charoset*, one of the traditional items eaten during the Seder service on the first night of Passover, or the fried *Matzah*, which is prepared as a dish for a meal during Passover week?

Charoset
8 oz. apples
2 oz. raisins
2 oz. almonds or walnuts
Cinnamon
A small amount of sweet wine

Peel and core the apples and then chop them finely with the nuts and raisins. Add the cinnamon to taste and then add the wine. Now mix the ingredients until they form a paste.

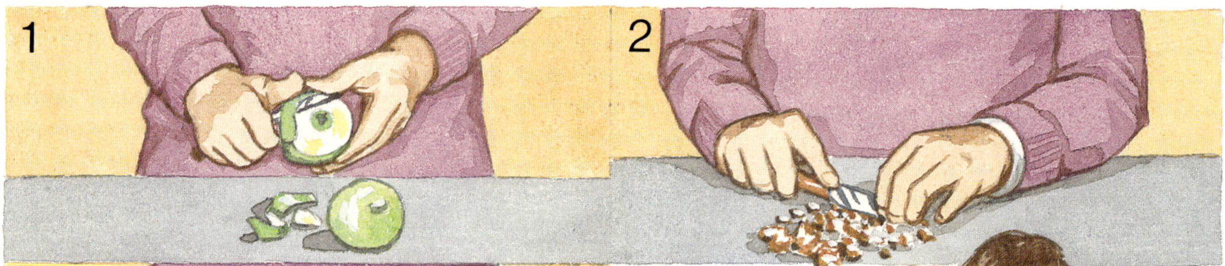

Charoset represents the cement and bricks used by the slaves in Egypt. You will find it tastes quite delicious – to Jews, its sweetness stands for God's constant kindness that made even the slavery bearable.

Fried *Matzah*

1 packet of *Matzah* (from a supermarket)
Grated lemon or orange rind
2 eggs
Vegetable fat or oil
Some milk, sugar and cinnamon

Break the *Matzah* into quarters and then soak the pieces in the milk until they are fairly soft but not soggy. Drain the *Matzah* and dip both sides in some beaten egg. Now fry both sides of the *Matzah* in the vegetable oil or fat until it is light brown in color. Serve the fried *Matzah* with sugar, cinnamon and grated lemon or orange rind.

Ask an adult to help you with these recipes before you start.

The Feast of Weeks

Seven weeks after the Passover festival comes another major celebration called the Feast of Weeks, Pentecost, or *Shavuot* in Hebrew, which occurs some time during May or June.

This festival commemorates the time when the *Torah* was given to Moses, on Mount Sinai. It also marked the beginning of the summer harvesting of wheat in the Holy Land, and the offering of the first fruit – wheat, barley, grapes, figs, pomegranates, olives and dates – during the time when there was a holy place, called the Temple, in Jerusalem. These seven fruits were given to the Priests of the Temple, who had no land of their own, as a gift as well as a thanksgiving offering to God.

On this festival the Jewish place of worship, the synagogue, is decorated with flowers and greenery in order to remind the Jews of the lush vegetation around Mount Sinai at the time the *Torah* was given to Moses, as well as the agricultural nature of the festival. It also recalls that Moses was placed in a cradle of green bulrushes when he was a baby, and put into the Nile River to save him from being drowned along with other Israelite boys at the command of the Pharaoh. It links the past with the present in the long chain of Jewish history.

This picture by the famous painter, Rembrandt, shows Moses holding the stone tablets containing the Ten Commandments, which he received on Mount Sinai from God.

Shavuot is rather different from the other two Pilgrim Festivals – Passover and Tabernacles – as it lasts for only two days (one day in Israel), whereas the other two are eight-day festivals. On this festival, the biblical Book of Ruth is read publicly in the synagogue, as its central theme takes place at the time of the harvest.

So on this important celebration, Jews remember two outstanding characters of the Bible – Moses, a symbol of man's greatness, and Ruth, the symbol of feminine devotion and gentleness.

Children in Israel celebrating the time when God gave Moses the Torah.

The *Torah*

When Moses led the Israelites out of Egypt, they left as a free people. But a free person still has to have discipline, rules and regulations in order to know how to live a good life and behave in the correct manner. These laws, or commandments, were given to Moses on Mount Sinai and became known in Hebrew as the *Torah*, or the Five Books of Moses. This word has no exact translation in any other language, because it includes not only

Central to any synagogue is the Holy Ark in which is housed the Torah *scrolls. The Rabbi standing next to the Ark of this French synagogue is holding the* Torah *scrolls.*

These Torah *scrolls were handwritten over two hundred years ago.*

laws of conduct, the rights of the individual, the festivals, offerings to the priests, and the Sabbath, but is also about how the world came into being, about Adam and Eve, the Patriarchs Abraham, Isaac and Jacob and their families, as well as other characters who appeared at the dawn of civilization.

So really the word *Torah* can best be translated into English as "teaching." The original Hebrew words in every *Torah* are written by a trained scribe with a quill pen and specially prepared ink onto a scroll of parchment. When completed, the scroll is considered as a holy object and must be treated with respect.

However, the scroll containing the Five Books of Moses is written in a shortened form, and in order to understand the real meaning of its words and its message, a vast amount of discussion on every letter and every word took place among the early Rabbis over hundreds of years. All the discussions and decisions were put into a set of holy books called the *Talmud*, coming from the Hebrew word meaning "to study."

From generation to generation, these laws have been studied and observed. From Mount Sinai, some 3,300 years ago, to this very day, Jews have accepted the commandments of the *Torah* as their guide throughout their lives. On the Pilgrim Festival of *Shavuot*, this is commemorated and celebrated by Jews throughout the world.

The Feast of Tabernacles

The third of the Pilgrim Festivals is called the Feast of Tabernacles or *Succot*. This is a happy festival and many families build a *Succah* (a booth or hut) in their gardens. Each *Succah* is made out of wood or some other suitable material, with a roof of bamboo sticks or pine branches. These temporary dwellings are often built in synagogues for congregations to enjoy.

Succot reminds Jews of the time the Israelites lived in huts during their wanderings for nearly forty years in the Wilderness before reaching the

Building a Succah *in the garden.*

A Succot *celebration in Israel.*

Holy Land to become an independent nation. During the week of the festival, meals are eaten in the *Succah*, and some people even sleep there during the whole of Tabernacles week.

Like the other two Pilgrim Festivals, *Succot* is also an agricultural festival. It is celebrated during the months of September and October, which is after the crops have been harvested. A branch of a palm tree, a citron (a fruit that looks very much like a lemon), three myrtle branches and two willow branches are used during the morning services as symbols of the agricultural aspect of the festival.

The festival has another name, The Season of Our Rejoicing. In the past, Jews gave thanks to God for the harvested crop by rejoicing and celebrating around the Temple in Jerusalem for seven days.

A Joyous Celebration

For a few moments let us go back in time to the days when the Holy Temple stood in Jerusalem. Thousands of pilgrims had come from all parts of the land to celebrate the festival of *Succot*, and on the eve of the second day a most exciting and beautiful ceremony took place. It was called "The Celebration of the Water Drawing." The Priests together with their assistants led the long procession to the well outside the city of Jerusalem, to the accompaniment of musical instruments and songs of praise to God.

This sight was so spectacular, dignified and moving that it has been said: "He who has not seen The Celebration of the Water Drawing has not seen a real celebration in his life."

The Temple Court, which had separate sections for men and women, was brilliantly

A model of the second Temple. The actual Temple was built in Jerusalem 2,500 years ago and it replaced one built 1,000 years earlier and later destroyed.

illuminated and on each of the fifteen steps leading from one court to the other, certain psalms were chanted. The streets were lit by people in the procession carrying flaming torches, and when they arrived at the well they drew water and brought it to the Temple. There the Priests poured it onto the altar.

This joyous celebration is commemorated these days by having special food and drink in the *Succah*, and singing songs from the Bible and the Prayer Book. The last day of the festival of *Succot* is called "The Rejoicing of the Law," or *Simchat Torah* in Hebrew, and it marks the end of the yearly cycle of readings from the *Torah*. The *Torah* scrolls are carried seven times around the synagogue, with children carrying colorful flags following the procession, accompanied by religious songs and dances.

A procession of Jewish children celebrating The Rejoicing of the Law, Simchat Torah.

The Festival of Lights

On the three Pilgrim Festivals, considered as the major Jewish festivals, normal weekday activities such as going to work, to school and to the office are not allowed. However, on the minor festivals, such as "The Festival of Lights," or *Chanukah*, such activities are permitted, but special prayers, symbols and reminders of the event that is being commemorated are carried out or used. *Chanukah* falls in December.

The main *Chanukah* symbol is a lamp called a *Chanukiyah*, which holds eight candles. The festival lasts for eight days, and on each night a candle is lit – one the first evening, two the next night, and so on until all eight are alight on the final night. It is for this reason that the eight days are known as The Festival of Lights. The word *Chanukah* actually comes from the Hebrew word meaning "dedicate," so this festival is also known as "The Festival of Dedication."

On the last night of Chanukah, *all eight candles in the* Chanukiyah *are lit.*

The event that is being celebrated happened over 2,000 years ago. The king of Syria at that time was Greek, and he issued a command forbidding the Jews to keep their religious beliefs and way of life. Eventually, a small number of Jews rebelled against the Syrian soldiers and were victorious in their fight. In the meantime, the Temple in Jerusalem had been desecrated by the enormous army of the Syrians, and when the

Jewish warriors came to clean the Temple, they could find only one cruse (a small, earthenware container) of oil with the seal of the High Priest on it. The cruse of oil was used to light the seven-branched candlestick, called the *Menorah*, in the Temple. Normally, this cruse of oil would have lasted only for one day, but miraculously it kept alight for eight days, by which time new holy oil had been prepared and the Temple was rededicated to the service of God. So it is easy to see why this minor festival is called both The Festival of Lights and The Festival of Dedication.

The eight days of the festival are reminders of the victory over the Syrian king, whose command would have destroyed the very soul and spirit of the Jewish people. The special psalms and songs sung by Jews during this week express thanksgiving, not for victory in war, but for being able to continue to worship God according to His commandments, and being able to practice the religion of their fathers.

A Chanukah *service in the synagogue of Jerusalem's Hadassa Hospital. The windows of the Tribes of Israel, by the famous artist Marc Chagall, can also be seen.*

The Words of the Prophet Zechariah

The hero of the *Chanukah* story is a Priest called Mattathias. He had the courage to stand up against the Greek king of Syria because he felt that a human being should be completely free. To give up his Judaism and be forced to accept Greek thought and custom, as well as worship the Greek god Zeus, would have meant being a slave to the orders of the Syrian king, and giving up the freedom of being a Jew.

This old picture shows Judah the Maccabee pursuing the Syrian forces.

A giant outdoor Chanukiyah *at a* Chanukah *party.*

Together with his five sons and a small group of followers, Mattathias defied the orders of the Syrians and began a war that was to last for several years. Finally, it was the son of Mattathias, Judah the Maccabee, who led the Jews to a victory over the enormous number of soldiers who were ordered to stamp out the Jewish religion.

Throughout the generations, Jews have been reminded of the words of the Prophet Zechariah: "... it is not with armed forces and not with power but with my spirit, says the Lord." This reminder is done in a very obvious way – by the lighting of the *Chanukah* candles on the eight nights of the festival. Jews believe that the message of the Prophet's words is of importance for all time and for all mankind: that force and power cannot destroy belief, faith and trust in God and in people.

In modern Israel, a giant *Chanukiyah* lit by electric lights can be seen illuminating the top of every large or public building, including the Israeli parliament, the *Knesset.* You can imagine the beautiful scene created by the lights from the windows and the tops of buildings on these long winter nights. Children play special games and eat delicious jam-filled doughnuts or potato pancakes all fried in oil, to recall the small cruse of oil found in the Temple.

The Feast of Lots

We have to go back many centuries to ancient Persia (now called Iran) to learn the story of *Purim*. At one time, the Prime Minister of King Ahasuerus, a man called Haman, decided to kill all the Jews in Persia, just because Mordechai, who was a Jew, would not bow down to Haman when he entered the palace. So Haman tricked the

Fancy dress parties are a popular part of the Purim *celebrations. In Israel, colorful street parades are commonplace.*

This parchment scroll is called the Scroll of Esther, or Megillah. *It is read out in the synagogue during* Purim.

King into issuing a decree to kill all the Jews living in his country, and Haman cast lots (a kind of raffle) to decide the date when this horrible decree should be carried out.

Fortunately, the Jews had a friend in the palace in the person of Queen Esther, who was herself Jewish and the niece of Mordechai. The date set for the slaughter of the Jews was the thirteenth of the Hebrew month of Adar (around March), and the Queen arranged a number of banquets long before that date inviting both the King and Haman to attend.

During the last of the banquets, she exposed Haman's plot to the King explaining that she, too, would have to be killed as she was Jewish. The King was furious that his Prime Minister had tricked him into issuing the decree, and ordered that Haman and his sons be hanged on the very gallows Haman had put up for Mordechai. At the same time, the King withdrew the decree and appointed Mordechai as Prime Minister.

To celebrate this miraculous saving of Jewish lives, a minor festival was established known as *Purim,* which is Hebrew for the word "lots," when the whole episode is read publicly in the synagogue from a parchment scroll – the Scroll of Esther. During the reading, whenever the name of Haman is mentioned, all the children try to drown out his name by banging hammers, shaking rattles and other noisemakers, blowing whistles or by just hissing and stamping their feet.

Things to do

Two items used on *Purim* are the Scroll of Esther, or *Megillah* in Hebrew, and a noisemaker, which is also known as a "greggar." Here are some simple instructions on how to make these two items.

The Scroll of Esther

Things you will need:
A box of wax paper
A flat stick
Acrylic paint
Strong glue
Marker pens

Remove the metal cutting edge from a box of wax paper. Cut holes in the ends of the box, large enough to expose the end of the cardboard tube and the roll of wax paper, and then paint the outside of the box so that it is bright and colorful. When the paint is dry, glue the stick to the inside of the cardboard tube and let it dry. (The stick will be used to reroll the scroll.) Now unroll the wax paper, use the marker pens to illustrate scenes from the Book of Esther in the Bible, and write in descriptions of the scenes.

The Noisemaker

Things you will need:
Dried beans or rice
Two aluminum foil plates
A stapler or tape
Marker pens

Place a handful of dried beans or rice on one of the foil plates. Then place the second plate over the first and staple or tape them together. Use the marker pens to draw the face of Haman. Now shake the noisemaker or hit it with your fingers – it will make plenty of noise!

The Jewish New Year

The Ten Days of Repentance

In the Jewish calendar there is a period of ten days that are neither joyous nor sad. Days that do not celebrate a good harvest or recall a historic event. These special days, which are more serious than the other Holy Days, concern the life of the individual Jew. During these days, every Jew pauses to think if he or she can change to become a better, kinder and more considerate human being. This period of ten days is known as the "Ten Days of Repentance," or the "Ten Days of Return."

The Ten Days of Repentance begins the Jewish New Year, called *Rosh Hashanah* in Hebrew, which occurs around September. Jews spend their time during the two days of this occasion mainly in the synagogue, with the morning services lasting about five hours. The evening services are quite short, and during the meal that follows, some of the bread, called *Challah*, is dipped into honey to symbolize a "good, sweet year." During the daytime services in the synagogue, the Rabbi and the Cantor (who conducts the prayers) wear white as a sign of purity to commence the New Year with a fresh start. It is also a reminder of the seriousness of the day.

During the Rosh Hashanah *services, the* Shofar *is blown.*

During the services, the Ram's Horn or *Shofar* is blown. The shrill sound moves the congregation to repent and mend their ways, and acts as a call for greater concentration on the prayers. In the Bible, the New Year is called "The Day of the Sounding of the *Shofar.*" The sound of the *Shofar* has been used since biblical times on important and historical occasions.

Jews greet each other during this period with the words, *"Shanah Tovah,"* which means "a good year." They also offer prayers to God and extend good wishes to family and friends.

During Rosh Hashanah, *Jews spend much of their time in the synagogue.*

A Time for Reflection

In the various prayers, the New Year is known as the "Day of Memorial" and the "Day of Judgment" for two reasons. First, it reminds Jews of the Creation of the world, which is believed to have taken place on this date. And second, because Jews believe that people are judged by God, according to their past deeds and their prayers during this period, for the coming year – who will live, who will die, who will have a good life and who will survive in misery.

The main purpose of the Ten Days of Repentance, however, is for Jews to reflect on their lives and examine themselves. The Hebrew word for repentance, *Teshuvah,* comes from a word meaning "return" – to return to God and his teachings. Before asking God to pardon any sins that may have been committed during the past year, the Jew has first of all to ask forgiveness for any wrong done to another human being, and

A Rosh Hashanah *celebration dinner at a* kibbutz *in Israel.*

Jews studying mystical books on the New Year.

only after that has been put right, and pardon given, can he or she appear before God and promise to return to the good ways of the *Torah*.

The New Year is a time when each and every Jew must try to turn over a new leaf, and not make the same mistakes as in the past. Resolutions are made that will improve everything connected with life. In other words they take stock of the way they act, speak, think and behave in their daily lives. If they feel that they can think and behave in a better way, they must make the effort in the coming year to do just that and thereby live a life in accordance with the ideals of the *Torah*.

Although *Rosh Hashanah* is a solemn occasion, there is a place for joy as well. After being able to say, "I made a mistake. I am sorry," and repenting and resolving to improve, the Jew is confident that God will show His mercy and judge him favorably.

The Day of Atonement

The last day of the Ten Days of Repentance – the Day of Atonement or *Yom Kippur* – is the most important and holy day in the Jewish calendar. It is a day when no work is allowed, no food is eaten, nor liquid drunk. The day is spent in the synagogue in various forms of prayer, listening to portions of the Bible read out of a *Torah* scroll and sermons given by the Rabbi. All of these activities and the avoidance of any bodily pleasure for twenty-five hours are meant to lead to sincere repentance and to be atoned or "at one" with God the Creator.

On the eve of this special day, the service begins with the two words *Kol Nidrei*, which the Cantor chants in a melody that is both beautiful and sad. The sound of this haunting theme – sung in every synagogue and Jewish place of worship throughout the world – brings to mind the persecutions and sufferings endured by the Jewish people over the centuries. But it is also a hymn of hope and faith in the eternity of Judaism and all that it has given to civilization.

The synagogue is fully lit with every possible light shining, as a message of hope and brightness. White curtains and table covers give an added feeling of purity and righteousness – all creating an atmosphere that helps those present to repent and to resolve to improve themselves.

The long day ends with the concluding service,

This Torah *scroll being displayed by a Tunisian Rabbi is more than 1,300 years old.*

called *Ne'eelah,* which takes place as the sun sets. So comes to an end the ten days of prayer, study and thoughts of improvement by young and old alike. *Yom Kippur* has been spent in hunger and thirst and remembrance of the past with a promise to do better and a hope that all will be forgiven. The past year is closed and the coming year and the future is what is now important. The day has come and gone and finally closes with the shrill sound of the *Shofar.*

A service in a synagogue. On Yom Kippur, *the day is spent in the synagogue.*

New Year for Trees

It may sound strange that trees should have a New Year or a birthday, but in the Jewish religion trees are very important as a symbol of life. In the Bible a person is compared to a tree, and in a number of King David's psalms, a majestic and fruit-laden tree is compared to a person who does good deeds.

This minor festival, called *Tu Bishvat* in Hebrew, takes place on the fifteenth day of the Hebrew month of *Shevat* – in January or February. This is the time when the winter season ends and the sap of the tree becomes active again, bringing new life from the roots to the branches and twigs. This date was fixed for the purpose of bringing tithes, or offerings, to the Temple in Jerusalem, and also for deciding the laws for the Sabbatical Year when new fruit was not allowed to be eaten for a whole year.

In the Holy Land, trees are very important as they give shade in the hot climate, they provide food in the form of fruit, and they provide timber for building purposes. For over eighty years, Jews from all over the world have given small contributions to the Jewish National Fund, making it

Picking oranges on a kibbutz. *Trees are important in Israel, not only for the fruit they provide, but for the shade they give and timber they provide.*

possible to plant millions of trees in Israel – to provide picnic areas and to develop land in the desert and on mountain tops. During the festival, schoolchildren, who are given saplings by this organization to plant, recite a special blessing as they place the roots of the saplings into the soil.

Israeli children planting saplings on Tu Bishvat. *Many of the trees planted on this festival are provided by the international organization, the Jewish National Fund.*

By observing this minor festival, Jews show their faith in the future and in the day when, as the Bible says, everyone will be able to sit under his own fig tree and be unafraid. Various types of fruit are eaten on this day. Some people try to eat as many as fifteen different kinds of fruit – equal in number to the date of the month – especially those fruits that they have not eaten before. A prayer is recited when a fruit is eaten for the first time in the season.

Israel's Independence Day

On November 29, 1947, the United Nations General Assembly in New York adopted the resolution to establish the modern State of Israel. On May 14, 1948, the new state was proclaimed – the Jewish people now had a homeland for the first time in 2,000 years. This day corresponds to the Hebrew date of 5 Iyar, and since that time it has been observed as Israel's Independence Day or *Yom Ha'tzmaut.*

For only the first few years, military parades formed an important part of the Independence Day celebrations.

On this day, special prayers of thanksgiving are said in synagogues, because Jews had prayed for centuries for a return to their own land.

Many Jews lost their lives after the Jewish state had been established through a number of wars with their neighbors. These soldiers are remembered on the day before Independence Day in Israel.

At the end of this sad day, sirens give the signal for the closing of Remembrance Day and the beginning of the Independence Day celebrations. All over Israel there are firework displays, music and dancing, and the streets are full of people singing and creating a happy and jolly atmosphere.

Street dancing in Jerusalem on Independence Day.

Between Passover and Pentecost

Israeli soldiers rejoicing at Jerusalem's Western Wall after the city had become reunited, in June 1967.

Besides Israel's Independence Day, there are three other important minor festivals between the two major festivals of Passover and Pentecost. The first commemorates an event that happened over 2,000 years ago, and is known as the Thirty-third Day of Omer, or *Lag Ba'omer* in Hebrew. The "omer" was a measure of grain, which was brought to the Temple in Jerusalem daily for the forty-nine days between the major festivals, as an offering. It was on the thirty-third day, many centuries ago, that a plague that had been raging suddenly ceased. Ever since that day, fun outdoor activities, such as games and picnics, are arranged in remembrance of the miracle.

Ten days after *Lag Ba'omer*, a more modern period of history is celebrated. This occasion is Jerusalem Day, *Yom Yerushalayim*, when during the Six-Day War in 1967 Jerusalem once again became a united city after having been divided into two sections in 1948. When the city was reunited, the first thing the soldiers did was to flock to the only remaining part of the Temple of old, known as the Western Wall, *Kotel Ma'aravee*. Jews throughout the world offered prayers of thanks to God for having caused Jerusalem to be reunited and for making it possible to visit the Western Wall once again.

Jerusalem Day at the Western Wall. Services and celebrations are a feature of this festival.

Annual services and celebrations are organized on this day, not only in Jerusalem and throughout Israel, but in any region where a number of Israeli Jews live. In this way, Jews remember the Jerusalem of the past – its tragedy and loss, its history and victory – and look forward to the future.

Perhaps the newest holiday is *Yom Hasho'ah*, or Holocaust Day. This holiday commemorates the six million Jews who died in the Holocaust and honors those who survived. It is celebrated in Israel on May 6, the day that Allied troops liberated Buchenwald, the first Nazi concentration camp.

The Sabbath

The Sabbath begins on Friday evening. Candles are lit to mark the start of the day, and before the evening meal begins, blessings are said over wine and specially braided bread.

The most important holiday for Jews is the weekly Sabbath, or *Shabbat* in Hebrew, occurring on Saturdays. One would think that having a special day every week would not be something that brings excitement and satisfaction. But for Jews this is not the case at all, as the Sabbath is the only holiday mentioned in the Ten Commandments.

This special holy day commences like all other Jewish occasions – on the evening of the day

A boy reading a passage from the Torah *during his* Bar Mitzvah. *This and other special ceremonies take place on the Sabbath.*

before. So on Friday evening, the mother of the household ushers in the Sabbath by reciting a blessing and lighting candles after having placed some money in a charity box, remembering those who are less fortunate, and commencing this different kind of day by carrying out the commandment of giving charity.

Once the candles have been lit, all normal weekday work and activity stops. This is a day set apart from the usual routine. It is a time for prayer, for meals around the family table accompanied by the singing of special Sabbath-day hymns, for study and for visiting family and friends.

Everything carries on at a much slower pace than during the rest of the week. Jews have time to discuss, to chat, to relax and to remember that a person is not a slave but a servant of God, and that by carrying out His laws they can become kind, generous, considerate and happy.

Adults and children attend the synagogue services where they not only pray, listen to the reading of the *Torah* scroll and hear a sermon by the Rabbi, but also share in the joys and sorrows of the congregation. Special ceremonies such as a *Bar Mitzvah* – a ceremony that marks a boy's entry into adulthood at the age of thirteen – takes place on the Sabbath. Announcements are made regarding births, forthcoming weddings, a recovery from illness or a bereavement. So all give comfort to the sad and rejoice with the happy.

The Jewish Calendar

The Jewish calendar is based on the movements of the sun and moon, and because of this the dates of the months vary from year to year. Normally there are twelve calendar months beginning with *Tishri*, the month of the Jewish New Year. This occurs around autumn time, during the months of September and October. In a Jewish leap year, another month of *Adar* is added, making thirteen calendar months instead of twelve.

Calendar months	Jewish festivals
Tishri *(Sept – Oct)*	The New Year *(Rosh Hashanah)* *2 days* The Day of Atonement *(Yom Kippur)* *1 day* The Feast of Tabernacles *(Succot)* *8 days* The Rejoicing of the Law *(Simchat Torah)* *1 day*
Cheshvan *(Oct – Nov)*	
Kislev *(Nov – Dec)*	The Festival of Lights *(Chanukah)* *8 days*
Teveth *(Dec – Jan)*	
Shevat *(Jan – Feb)*	New Year for Trees *(Tu Bishvat)* *1 day*
Adar *(Feb – March)*	The Feast of Lots *(Purim)* *1 day*
Nisan *(March – April)*	Passover *8 days*
Iyar *(April – May)*	Holocaust Day *(Yom Hasho'ah)* Israel's Independence Day *(Yom Ha'atzmaut)*
Sivan *(May – June)*	Thirty-third Day of Omer *(Lag Ba'omer)* *1 day* Jerusalem Day *(Yom Yerushalayim)* *1 day* The Feast of Weeks (Pentecost/*Shavuot)* *2 days*
Tamuz *(June – July)*	
Av *(July – Aug)*	
Ellul *(Aug – Sept)*	

The Hebrew Alphabet

Hebrew is the official language of Israel. It has its own alphabet or *alef-bet* as it is called in Hebrew. Here are the letters of the Hebrew alphabet and how they are pronounced. A letter marked with a "✻" is silent when it is used without vowel signs. A letter marked with a "★" is written differently when it appears at the end of a word. You should read the alphabet and words from right to left.

ה H	ד D	ג G	ב V	בּ B	✻ א
כּ K	י Y	ט T	ח CH	ז Z	ו V
✻ ע	ס S	★ נ/ן N	★ מ/ם M	ל L	★ כ/ך CH
שׁ SH	ר R	ק K	★ צ/ץ TS	★ פ/ף F	פּ P
Vowel signs and dots occur mostly under the letters, sometimes inside or above them. The capital letters in the words below the signs or dots show how the vowels should be pronounced. (The circles are not a part of the alphabet. They are a positional guide only.)				ת T	שׂ S

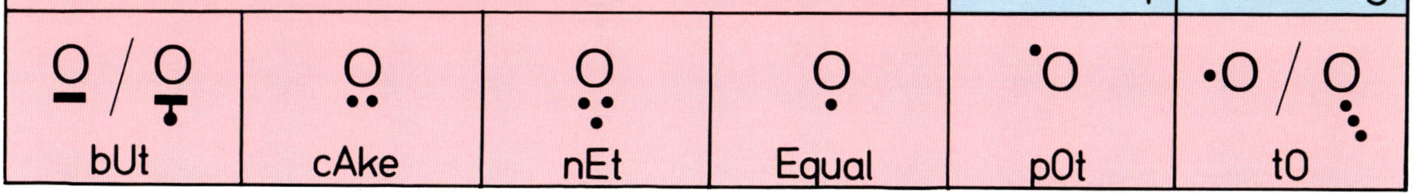

Here are a few Hebrew words written in their original form. From the alphabet, try to work out how they are pronounced – the answers are on page 48. (A letter with two vertical dots beneath it has no vowel – the letter is pronounced by its natural sound.)

1. שָׁלוֹם means "hello," "goodbye" or "peace."

2. לְהִתְרָאוֹת means "see you later," or "cheerio."

3. תּוֹדָה means "thank you."

4. בְּבַקָּשָׁה means "please," or "that's all right."

Glossary

Atonement An act that makes amends for sins committed – to restore the proper relationship between God and people.

Cantor A person who leads the prayers in a synagogue. He is usually chosen for his fine singing voice, as most prayers are chanted or sung.

Chanukiyah A lamp that holds eight candles. It is used during the Festival of Lights, or *Chanukah* in Hebrew.

Exodus The departure of the Israelites from Egypt led by Moses.

Hebrew The ancient language of the Jews, and now the official language of modern Israel.

Israelites The ancient name for the Jews.

Matzah Square, wafer-like biscuits eaten during Passover.

Patriarch The father and ruler of a family or tribe.

Rabbi A religious teacher and leader and the chief official in a synagogue.

Synagogue The Jewish place of worship and meeting.

Torah This can have several meanings, and in this book is used to refer to the holy scroll in which is written the revealed will of God. The *Torah* is also known as The Five Books of Moses, or the Pentateuch.

Further Reading

If you would like to find out more about Jewish festivals and the Jewish religion, you may like to read the following books:

The Hanukkah Book by Marilyn Burns (Four Winds Press, 1981)

Light Another Candle: The Story and Meaning of Hanukkah by Miriam Chaikin (Clarion, 1981). Other books by the same author include *Shake a Palm Branch: The Story and Meaning of Sukkot*, and *Sound the Shofar: The Story and Meaning of Rosh Hashanah and Yom Kippur.*

Judaism by Meyer Domnitz (Watts, 1986)

Hanukkah: Eight Nights, Eight Lights by Malka Drucker (Holiday House, 1980). Other books by the same author include *Passover: A Season of Freedom, Rosh Hashanah and Yom Kippur: Sweet Beginnings, Shabbat: A Peaceful Island*, and *Sukkot: A Time to Rejoice.*

I Am a Jew by Clive Lawton (Watts, 1985)

Index

Answers to page 45: 1. *Shalom* 2. *L'hitraot* 3. *Todah* 4. *B'vakasha*

Acknowledgments

The publisher would like to thank all those who provided pictures on the following pages: Mary Evans Picture Library 4; Sally & Richard Greenhill 5, 9; Sonia Halliday Photographs 10, 34; JNF Education Department 7: Jewish Programme Materials Project 15, 20, 27, 33, 37, 38, 39, 40, 41; The Mansell Collection 6, 8, 24; PHOTRI 31, 35; Picturepoint Ltd. 14, 32, 36; Ronald Sheridan's Photo-Library 16, 17, 21, 25, 42; Rev. Reuben Turner filmstrip; *Judaism – A Way of Life* 30, 43; Malcolm S. Walker artwork 12, 13, 28, 29; ZEFA cover, 11, 18, 19, 22, 23, 26.

61 Western Road, Hove, East Sussex BN3 1JD, England